Architecture of the New West:

Recent Works by Cottle Graybeal Yaw Architects

First published in the United States of America in 2002 by:
The Ashley Group
2002 Clearwater Drive
Oak Brook, IL 60523
630.288.7901

Copyright 2002 Cottle Graybeal Yaw Architects
Post Office Box 529
Basalt, CO 81621

www.cgyarchitects.com

tel 970-927-4925
fax 970-927-8578

email aspen@cgyarchitects.com

Distributed by:
W. W. Norton & Company, Inc.
500 Fifth Avenue
New York, NY 10110
212-354-5500; 212-869-0856 fax

Cottle, Graybeal, Yaw, CGY Architects
Architecture, Modern-20th Century- United States, Western Regional Architecture.
Colorado Architecture—Pictoral works
Cottle, Graybeal, Yaw. II. Title.
Library of Congress Control Number 2002107126

720 '02-dc 20

Front cover photo: David O. Marlow

Back cover photos: David O. Marlow, Pat Sudmeier

Contributing Writer: Patrick Soran

Printed in Hong Kong
10 9 8 7 6 5 4 3 2 1
ISBN: 1-58862-101-4

$39.95

Contents

Foreword 6

Introduction 10

Home 14

Sopris Mountain Ranch

Mintz Residence

Private Residence

Private Residence

Castle Creek Residence

Ramo Residence

Pinon Mesa Homestead

House at Wildcat Ridge

Private Residence

Powell Residence

Wright Residence

Private Residence

Schell Residence

Sopris Drive Residence

Smithburg Residence

Ryan Residence

Coleman Residence

Vision Hill

Community 80

Architects' Studio

Aspen Mountain Gondola

The Little Nell

Sundeck

New Sheridan Restaurant

River Run Village at Keystone Resort

Aspen Club

Redstone Parkside

Inn at Semiahmoo

Falling Leaf Lodge and the Chautauqua Center

Zephyr Mountain Lodge

Firm History 126

Acknowledgments 128

Foreword

By Joseph Giovannini

Architecture has negotiated the relationship between man and nature since the cave. But in the 20th century, when the machine invaded the garden in the form of hard-edged buildings, an intangible seam divided the modernist house from nature, and the eye could never quite make the two whole again. Architects schooled in abstraction and indoctrinated in the social ideals of mass production feared the visual sentimentalism of buildings that looked naturalistic. An architect could be modern or traditional: it was an either/or choice.

Cottle Graybeal Yaw Architects has mastered the inclusionary art of being both/and: like gardeners, they graft the seemingly opposed building species, the traditional and the modern, to generate new, vigorous architectural hybrids. Based in Colorado in the midst of an American culture that believes in the spiritual transcendence of nature, they design buildings whose open modernist plans and volumes reflect today's informal living patterns. But they also excerpt shapes from vernacular building types such as the cabin, silo and mine, and appropriate materials like fieldstone and timber directly from heroic Western landscapes. Rather than distilling their houses to a rudimentary shape or simple Brancusi-esque idea, they cultivate complexity, creating rich environmental mixes that send different, sometimes contradictory messages — old and new, industrial and agricultural, man-made and machine-produced. Though they may come west to refresh their souls by immersion in nature, their clients often bring a highly developed visual sensibility; they usually resist facile theming. The architects cultivate the visual complexity that is already in the eye of their clients.

In the houses and resort buildings that define their practice, the site is both motivator and generator. Nature in the West, especially in and near the Rockies, is big and powerful, and collectively the views, topography, and sky exercise a strong magnetic pull that extroverts designs that become chapels to nature: like altars, fireplaces anchor houses otherwise tugged by a field of divergent forces. The pure Euclidean forms easy for machines to fabricate cannot remain self-referential and undisturbed given the draw of the landscape. Sloping sites with multiple views facing different exposures force the geometries to relax. These usual topographies resist the notion of a unitary whole and encourage the fragmentation of designs in both plan and section. The sites challenge gridded, orthogonal rigidity and any notion of controlling axialities or symmetries. The geometries structuring the houses become peripatetic.

Composing their buildings in segments, the architects angle the parts to take advantage of the site's qualities and they vary the building's cross-section: they drop rooms down with the slopes, and lift ceilings to create proper amphitheaters for the panorama. But people can't look at a huge view all day long, and architects who want to connect people to nature also need to design for intimacy. Sometimes the best way to understand an aspen tree in all its seasons is a close-up view from the bathtub. CGY understands that the scale of a view — a bluff, mountain or a nearby stream — determines whether to frame it or leave it wide open. Buildings are optical lenses, and the precise adjustment of the aperture can bring qualities of nature into greater clarity. A

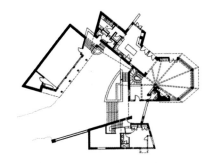

huge window, for example, may not be the best way to focus the view on snow. Sites in the West may seem indomitable, but CGY treats nature with sensitivity, knowing its perception is fragile.

But the architects cultivate more senses that just the eye. They sensualize buildings, capturing the acoustics of an adjacent stream, for example, by creating a courtyard that turns the house into a resonant acoustic envelope. To bring out a sense of rain, they use corrugated sheet metal on the roof to make the drops drum.

Informed by the logic of industrial production, modernists have usually operated by a process of subtraction, with architects distilling designs to an irreducible simplicity. In the context of a firm that specializes in one-of-a-kind buildings, CGY seems to have reversed the math, operating instead by a calculus and aesthetic of addition. Their design, however, is no less modernist, but simply pursues a different paradigm of modernism.

For CGY, the design strategy that has proved flexible enough to accommodate the many demands of their commissions is collage, a technique that involves layering and juxtaposing highly differentiated pieces and parts, often in unexpected ways. Instead of trying to make a unitary image fit diverse and often conflicting demands, the architects forego simplicity in favor of complexity, proliferating parts that retain a high degree of autonomy. The discipline that structures the design is not slavish regularity but a design

specificity intended to feature unique moments in the landscape or interior – an outcropping, a stand of trees, a distant peak, a window seat. As unforced and inevitable as their casual designs appear, the compositions are intricately puzzled together. The complexity is elegant and fitted rather than complicated.

CGY's clients are interested in connecting to nature, and the architects' palette, which ranges from field stone to barn siding to corrugated metal, is the most obvious means of establishing the bond. Together the textures form a unifying thread that ties the architectural compositions together. However, the architects also layer space when they layer materials. In the Coleman Residence, a porch built of heavy timbers supports a front facade of vertical wood siding; a first-story wall constructed of logs notched at their ends borders the back of the porch, and a short two-story stone tower beyond anchors the composition. Though they add to the painterly composition, the materials are never merely decorative but play a supporting role enclosing functional forms.

The architects may be taking from the palette of the old West, but they are also revealing the inherent natural beauty and texture of their materials. In the Mintz residence, the architects

push and pull the textured stone in a bas relief that adds deep noon-time shadows to the composition. They top the stone wall with corrugated metal roofing and allow it to rust: the resulting reddish-brown haze looks like a color-field painting, and its picturesque imperfection lends a sense of authenticity and age. In addition to the power of the firm's palette to connote local history, the materials substantiate the formal composition with a sense of mass. The feeling of weight, whether in stone or wood, contradicts the weightlessness that classically characterizes the volumetric composition of most modernist buildings. The buildings are grounded.

CGY frequently salts its palette with high-tech materials, throwing in the unexpected. The architects might contrast dry-stacked stone with patinaed steel surfaces or metal tie rods. Structural steel adds tension to the warm mix of woods set aglow by a late sun. A log set in front of a steel-sash window focuses attention on the bark's texture and irregularities. The apparent incongruity sparks an aesthetic energy.

The subtext of a natural palette is workmanship, and the hand that crafts these materials reinforces the building's tie to the environment. Fortunately, crafts people have been attracted to the areas where CGY works, and the architects can predicate their designs on workmanship that elsewhere is scarce. The stonemasons working on a home in Aspen, for example, each came to the job

with their own fingerprints, and to achieve an integrated, consistent texture, the architects rotated the masons every two hours. Few regions in America have the privilege of this problem.

CGY rarely borrows from the vernacular without reinventing it, and the architects develop the collagist sensibility of their designs by juxtaposing different building types in unusual combinations. In a private residence in Telluride, Colorado, they yoke a tower, barn and covered bridge in a unique composite of evocative forms. Calmed by the weathered siding and textured stonework, the daring typological collage looks historically plausible. The distant reference is the veduta done by Renaissance architects, who drew imaginary cityscapes composed of buildings relocated next to each other — though never in a farm context. Similarly, a house design in Eagle County, Colorado, looks like a small village, or a farm with many outbuildings — the happenstantial sequence of simple forms seems to have grown organically over time. Allowing themselves great syntactic freedom, the architects create plans with shock-absorbing capacity. The looseness of the whole allows the architects to inject the unexpected without throwing off the composition.

The site may set the parameters of what a house wants to be, but CGY clients often bring an additional set of expectations to their edenic getaways that affirm the complexities encouraged by the site. The family agenda itself

demands a flexibility that requires a house to expand and contract: the house teems during holidays and then shrinks back to more intimate moments when a single person takes a book over to the fireplace. Just as different windows orient to long and short views, the interior spaces, especially the public rooms, have a multiple scale. Building types with an agricultural pedigree, like barns, give the architects the square footage and volume of a great room appropriate for large family gatherings, and within these large spaces the architects shape subspaces for smaller groups and for individuals. A vacation house with more than a half-dozen bedrooms needs a gregarious room that still won't overwhelm a couple after all the children and grandchildren have left. The spatial collages the architects create inside give the interiors the multiple scales designed outside.

Whether with materials, forms, buildings types or scale, CGY works by a process that brings out the differences of the constituent parts. The architects tend not to blend the parts into homogenous wholes; they keep the language heterogeneous. Counterintuitively, though they may use traditional forms, the architects do not use them traditionally, but operate surgically on the geometries to open them to each other and to the outside in spatial flows. Often the architects carve the volumes, cutting them back to a state of incompletion, leaving angled forms and dynamically open sections. With a series of nested trapezoidal rooms, the flowing, open plan for stone-and-glass house on Vision Hill in Telluride is anything but what a composite of traditional forms would imply. Even the wooden bay window projecting from the solid stone wall is distorted. The Western we think we're watching reveals itself instead to be a German Expressionist film.

Despite the comfort levels achieved by the natural materials and the quotations from architectural tradition, the architects' formal design moves are boldly abstract. When the architects take traditional gables, and cut the angled slopes at a nonorthogonal angle, they transform both the tradition and the sense of traditionalism. While the geometries of many buildings are well behaved, others display a highly artistic modernist sensibility that puts to rest any hint of sentimentality. The abstraction is more obvious in certain projects, like the Ramo Residence, but it plays an active role in the design of almost all of their buildings. The breakdown of the classic barriers between the outdoor and indoor starts in plans that extend the architecture into nature and vice versa, in a reciprocal weave that lets residents feel that they always occupy nature.

Giving architectural form to the Aspen idea – the union of mind, body and spirit – is not an easy endeavor with an obvious solution. For CGY, the task of integrating man and nature through building involves both invention and borrowing, from the West and outside the West. The architects have devised an approach that opens traditionalism and modernism to each other so that they are not antagonistic but surprisingly supportive. The architects have hybridized the two traditions with an originality and rigor that are both a rarity and a pleasure.

Introduction

The 'New West' is a phenomenon as much as a physical place: it is a dynamically evolving rural-recreational lifestyle, blending work with play and creating new definitions of community. Families and businesses are relocating to small towns with cultural amenities in record numbers, and living with part-time residents who share allegiances between urban and rural communities. This latest western migration has generated an increasing appreciation for the land and passionate debates about its heritage and purpose: it is a wonderful time and place to practice architecture, to participate in the debate, and help form its future.

The West has inspired such legend that it is difficult to see where myth leaves off and reality begins. In fact, the western theme – whether in agriculture, governance, environmentalism, art, or everyday life – is the contrast between powerfully ingrained myths and the sometimes stark realities of culture, history, and the land.

Indestructibility is one of the West's greatest myths. Sadly, our history is one of exploitation and moving on. Now there is a new reality – we are settling in for the long term. This means a more interactive attitude about land, habits, and habitation, and active participation as stewards.

The interaction for us begins with questions: how do we respect this land, its past, people and culture, yet look forward? How can evolution respect heritage, embrace the possibilities of the present and future, and add meaning? What should this evolving habitation live like, feel like, and look like? Can architecture be topical and timeless at the same time? Each new project is an evolution from the last; however, the underpinnings, or principles, for our approach to architecture have remained unchanged:

Architecture is about connections. It is a process of discovering, developing, and strengthening connections – to the land, to our heritage, to a sense of surprise and joy, to a community, and most importantly, to each other.

Genuineness has great power. As our lives become increasingly 'virtual,' architecture has a sustaining ability to remind us of the actual and genuine qualities of the land, the light, the seasons, and of our domains. 'High-touch' connects us in time and place; it grounds us in here and now.

Architecture is most meaningful when it reflects the confluence of absolutely specific qualities: of a site, a family, a community, a situation. Attributes are tangible and intangible – the sound of water, orientation to a landmark, the color of an aspen grove, the smell of rain, a client's music. Specifics are the fundamental building blocks of a meaningful environment.

We have been privileged to work in sites of remarkable beauty, many inhabited for the first time. There is a responsibility inherent with bringing buildings into nature – it deserves great care. Responsive architecture ignites awareness, enhances the value inherent in natural sites, and is rejuvenating.

There is great joy in the act of discovery and creation.

When we founded our firm in Aspen, Colorado, we were introduced to the 'Aspen Idea,' a way of living that advocates an enriching union of intellectual, cultural, and recreational pursuits. The lifestyle created by fusing these attributes creates a 'wholeness' or 'connectedness' that resonated thirty years ago and today remains the common thread in our work, our clients, and explorations together.

To the creative clients who introduced us to their worlds, opened our eyes, and made this possible, we thank you.

John Cottle

Doug Graybeal

Larry Yaw

Rich Carr

14

Sopris Mountain Ranch

EMMA, COLORADO

Set in a high country amphitheater, this 3,000-square-foot home is characterized by the simplicity inherent in rural farm buildings. It explores sculptural forms derived from the regional context and the opportunities created between man-made and natural forms.

The home forms a courtyard containment within the surrounding landforms and a commonly found configuration in rural settlements wherein a series of building elements were constructed over time to meet the expanding needs of a growing family. Building forms and connecting stone walls define the internal courtyard space. The courtyard is manicured and tailored while outside the landscape remains completely natural.

An economy of means is evident in use of materials and color. Simple gable shed forms are clad in plywood with applied patterned battens; the roofing is corrugated steel from a local co-op. An overall whitewashing underscores spareness and speaks of civilization within the expansiveness and hues of nature.

Mintz Residence

VAIL, COLORADO

This house emphasizes a mountain architecture expressive of contemporary life while acknowledging the traditions and warmth of mountain materials. It is defined by contrasting opposites, as in the opposition of natural materials with tectonic ones; traditional with abstract forms.

The geometry of the home opposes the nature of the site. Where the site dips, the architecture rises; where countryside sweeps with broad swaths of rugged scenery, a stone base delineates between natural and manmade. The primary building masses form a bridge-connected "L," anchored into the hillside on the short leg and projecting towards sky and view on the longer leg. From the entry court, a stone wall erodes to create an opening, the first gesture to entry. Sequential planes of stone and glass unfold, transitioning from the rugged exterior to the refined character of interior volumes. Family spaces open to each other, organizing themselves beneath a single roof which recalls an agricultural form and is slightly tipped, opening to the expansive valley views. The plan creates a variety of exterior spaces to accommodate specific activities, however the vast majority of the wild site is left untouched.

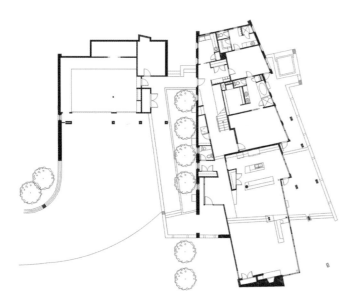

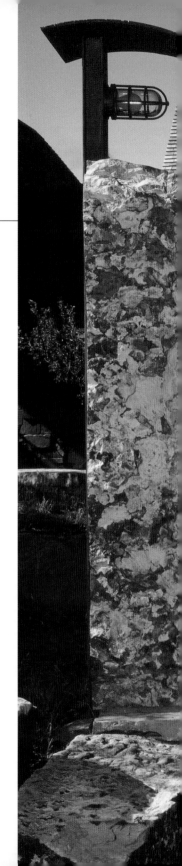

Private Residence

ASPEN, COLORADO

The clients wished to translate their affection for the character of rural Provence to a new home in Aspen. An exploration of this design challenge began with research into the historic architecture of these two diverse regions, producing several conceptual similarities: gathered building forms in working proximities; simple palettes of "site found" building materials; protected outdoor spaces defined by landforms; and buildings which evolved over time with economy of form and detailing.

The house's plan evolves around an exterior courtyard space that serves as entry court and outdoor "room." Three independent, yet variously connected stone building forms differentiate domains of the home and create a hilltown-like context.

The living room is the nucleus of the home and is organized around radial views and a large fireplace. Eroded from a massive stone wall, the fireplace is spanned by an 11-foot long stone lintel and layered inward. A plane of rusted steel creates inglenook seating emphasizing qualities of sanctuary and strength.

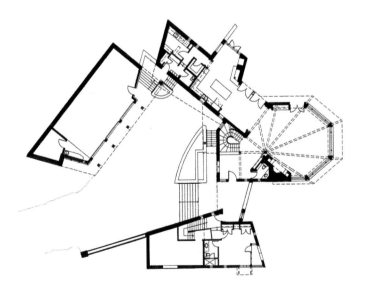

A simple palette of materials, predominantly stone, unifies the abstract geometries of the house.

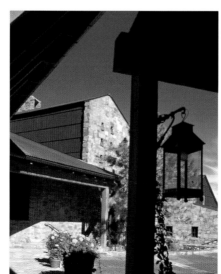

Separated roof forms tipped at unexpected angles shape interior spaces and sometimes overlap to provide shade and protection at the perimeter.

Private Residence

TELLURIDE, COLORADO

This house's iconic element – the bridge – is a creative solution to daunting site constraints. At grade, access is required at the lowest point on the site for ski-in and ski-out, but the most evocative site spaces are on the opposite end of the lot four floors above. The elevator and bridge also allow cars to pass under and create an auto court on the building's south side—advantageous in a location with snowy winters.

Using a concept evolved from mining forms, the home purposefully connects to Telluride's past. Historic mining buildings gathered together simple forms, memorable for their exaggerated verticality and powerful structures. Simple massing, the bridge truss, and over-scaled steel shingle siding recall these traditions.

Castle Creek Residence

ASPEN, COLORADO

Reconciling the divergent tastes of a modernist husband and his more traditionally oriented wife, this 4,000-square-foot home rejects the obvious blending of the two styles to instead establish a direct and purposeful confrontation. Derivative rural forms are grouped to create a more modern cluster of shapes around a courtyard. Gable forms are reduced to their most elemental, sculptural qualities; bay windows, a traditional prototype, become diagonal projections from the unembellished wall surface.

The house is situated above a small river on a mountainside bench invigorated by mature aspen groves and views to the high peaks of the Colorado Rockies. A low rubble-stone wall delineates a clear demarcation between constructed outdoor space and the surrounding natural environment; rusticated horizontal joints reinforce the metaphor of geologic strata. The floor plan clusters three separate and distinct "living cells," designed to be closed off for privacy and reflective of this pair of empty nesters' evolving family structure.

A white color palette derived from the surrounding aspen groves contrasts the stepped rubble stone base and highlights the clients' art collection.

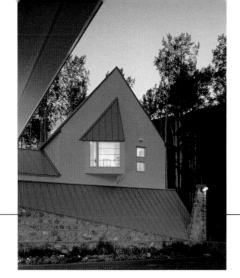

Using native sandstone and poured in place concrete, a rubble stone wall of varying heights surrounds and anchors the house at its base.

Ramo Residence

EAGLE COUNTY, COLORADO

The clients wanted a home with "the serenity of a Japanese tea house, the coziness of a Taos pueblo, and the uniqueness of Frank Lloyd Wright's prairie houses." Their site, blanketed with native scrub oak, juniper and sage, hugs a ridgeline overlooking distant mountain views. Merging design and site sensibilities, the house recreates the experience of walking along a ridge trail, where one alternately experiences the protection of oak groves and ridgeline exposure.

The qualities of the living spaces - how they connect to the site, the sense of enclosure or exposure - are varied, just as along the trail. The house is relaxed in places and explodes skyward in others, seemingly balanced between holding together and coming apart. This tension gives it great energy. A strong connection to the outdoors is dominant in every room; the cycles of weather and the changing of seasons become part of everyday experience in an informal, customary way.

Pinon Mesa Homestead

SOUTHEASTERN COLORADO

This house on a stone mesa is an interpretive response to inhabiting and integrating the high desert landscape. Broad horizontal roof forms rise from the earth to quietly echo the vast open landscape. Their serene repose is punctuated with more animated roof forms and towers to mark dominant spaces and to address desired views. Subtle historical references to ranch practices and Native American culture are woven into the forms and details.

The home site overlooks the vast expanse of an 82,000-acre ranch and the eastern slope of the Rocky Mountains. From its perch embracing the broad and distant vistas to the west, the house serves as both an overlook and a sanctuary from the harshness of the semi-arid climate. Corresponding to the degree of sanctuary, three courtyards enclose increasingly protected natural environments from native, to enhanced, to oasis.

House at Wildcat Ridge

SNOWMASS VILLAGE, COLORADO

Atop a mountain ridge, this isolated site has a tremendous variety of views, from rugged mountain vistas to intimate views of trees and a serene lake. Built for an industrial designer and his family, the home explores the idea of a glass house at 8,500-feet above sea level, where exposure to sun, snow and wind can be formidable.

The solution emerges as a series of contrasts: open vs. protected; industrial aeronautic references vs. historical mountain cabin; introverted vs. extroverted.

Distinct forms built of contrasting materials represent separate programmatic spaces which either frame or open to views and are organized to respect topography, sun orientation and view. A colored concrete base encompasses functional spaces such as garage and wine room and serves as a terrace floor interlocking the other forms of the building. Living and dining are the most extroverted spaces, contained in a single volume sheltered by a floating "wing" roof, allowing a curved glass curtain wall to embrace the most spectacular views. The kitchen is an introverted volume within the living space formed by a simple box to accommodate functional requirements. The bedrooms are articulated as gable-roofed volumes reminiscent of historical ranch cabins. The atrium, an organizing axis within the house, has structured fenestration on both walls creating a subtle transparency linking both sides of the ridge.

Private Residence

BOULDER, COLORADO

The clients wished to transform a poorly organized, older spec home into a new home synthesizing their lifestyle, contemporary art collection and desire to be environmentally sensitive.

A dramatic stainless steel stairway cuts through the center of the home and serves as the primary organizing element. An open floor plan takes advantage of lake and mountain views and engages the site with a range of outdoor spaces.

Focal points within the home, such as the stair, bar, and fireplace were designed as art objects. The cubist fireplace in the living area uses neon backlighting to lift an apparently floating surface off the back wall. The stairway is floated on columns enhancing its sculptural quality. A custom entry door opens onto the renovated entry revealing a sensuous, curved wood wall.

The owners and design team were committed to environmental responsibility. Nearly all materials removed from the existing home were recycled. Quick growth bamboo floors, durable stone flooring, natural wool carpets, VOC-free paints and stains, a high efficiency mechanical system, and an energy-saving light control system minimize environmental impact.

Powell Residence

TELLURIDE, COLORADO

Echoing its steep, rocky sandstone site, this house tumbles down a mountainside like a landslide in repose. The upper floors are anchored directly to bedrock while the lower levels rest on caissons drilled deep into alluvium deposits. Its geological narrative is further enhanced by use of native rock taken from the site, used on the exterior and interior of the home. The home and the surrounding natural rock create an acoustic envelope to enhance the sound of water as well as capture its visual playfulness.

The home responds to its larger environment as well. The plan concept, evolved from the idea of a hub and spokes, allows radiating living spaces and broad decks to look east toward Bridal Veil and Ingram Falls and west over Telluride.

Recycled barn siding and low maintenance recycled plastic decks reduce impact on the environment; heat mirror glass enhances energy efficiency; and, blown-in cellulose insulation is made from recycled newspaper.

Private Residence

SNOWMASS VILLAGE, COLORADO

Sited in a dense aspen grove, this home explores the idea of a tree house. A branch analogy is reflected abstractly and literally in the structural braces and is further developed in detailing in the cabinetry, hardware, and finishes.

The orthogonal colonnade holds space and composition together. Elements are broken off the orthogonal grid in response to specific needs such as orientation to outdoor activities, views, or topography. In essence, the house responds to site stimuli much like a tree would, accommodating existing conditions with maximum opportunity.

The material palette is purposefully simplified. The exterior is coursed stone veneer and 2 X 12 siding with log chinking; all interior wood is pine.

The placement and detailing of weathered steel rails, trim, light fixtures and fireplace remove reference to time or place.

Private Residence

EAGLE COUNTY, COLORADO

The owners' interest in the warmth and permanence of log structures became a springboard to conceive of the home as a series of cabins, with an emphasis on the spaces created between the cabins.

Sometimes enclosed, sometimes outdoors, these inter-building spaces are dynamic and very interactive with nature, responding to the owners' desire to be "connected to the land" rather than "looking at the view."

The cabins are traditional, simple forms executed in stone or square log construction. A light and airy "connective tissue," rendered almost entirely with window wall and timber framing, defines the in-between spaces, accentuating the indoor-outdoor interaction and emphasizing the solid nature of the cabins. The living room, bounded by three cabins and enclosed by the glazed connective tissue, has the quality of an outdoor space. Nature flows through the house in a series of outdoor terraces, gardens, and watercourses.

Schell House

TELLURIDE, COLORADO

A modern sensibility interprets mountain living while fulfilling the clients' desire for color, art, play and nature.

Entering the residence begins a journey of discovery, passing from the intimacy of the entrance hall, past a pair of sandblasted glass panels, and into the soaring, light-filled living room with its view of the San Sophia mountain range. Anchoring the main living space is a 25-foot high monoblock fireplace sheathed in warmly gleaming zinc; the starting point for the modernist vocabulary of radiating curves and angles.

On the open second level a steel handrail encloses a balcony. Just beyond, a frosted glass barn door alternately provides privacy or views of mountains from the master bedroom.

Materials such as maple and purple-heart wood, clear and frosted glass, pre-weathered zinc and brushed stainless steel, complement the palette of colors chosen to represent Colorado sunsets. Steel railings, sandblasted glass panels, and the zinc fireplace integrate with sculpture and paintings to become part of the art collection.

A playful approach incorporates exterior gable roofs to create a hidden observatory in the son's bedroom and is also expressed in an indoor, spray-on concrete climbing wall.

The purple-heart curve in the floor
mirrors the radiused dropped soffit
and works in conjunction with pre-
weathered zinc in the kitchen
backsplash and at the fireplace to
draw the eye through spaces.

Sopris Drive House

BASALT, COLORADO

Situated in a vintage neighborhood of mixed grain in a small Colorado town, the site was once part of a dairy farm and included a small Victorian house and work sheds in various states of disrepair. The clients wanted to undertake a complete remodel to reflect both the heritage of place as well as their modernist tastes.

Edged by mature trees, the narrow shape of the site with its gently terraced landforms resulted in a "linear compound" with an existing shed retained as a separating element between a new caretaker structure and the remodeled main house. A canopy of trees and a path of sandstone slabs leads to a glazed entry piece conceived as a garden "lantern" illuminating interior spaces. Focal points of the minimalist interiors, including the fireplace and curved entry wall, were created from raw patina steel.

A primary resolve of the client was to use off-the-shelf products from the local lumberyard or standard catalogues. A design precept of using common materials in uncommon ways resulted in plywood cabinets with saw cut face design; multiple paint colors on dry wall surfaces; board and batten plywood ceilings; and cementitious exterior siding. In recognition of heritage, exterior colors derive from the original structures.

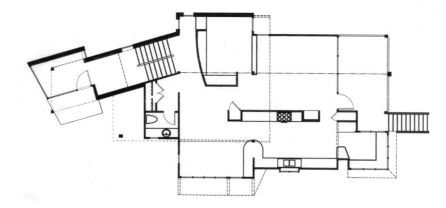

Several steel surfaces were placed as "guides" leading to the living room fireplace, also sculpted out of patina steel, where only fire and steel are expressed.

Smithburg Residence

ASPEN, COLORADO

This house is a direct response to the owners' desire for a home with "modernist sensibilities, Old World roots and an ambiguity of interpretation." The modernist character is strongly established by plan and building forms, and further manifested in angled window projections, raw steel columns, and connective detail. The contrasting traditional character is most strongly seen in the use of "old world" stone walls and exposed heavy-timber structural and trellis elements.

The project is organized around a 200-foot-long stone wall which aligns axially with a forested view of Mount Sopris to the west. The wall symbolically divides program functions between public and private while allowing the surrounding environment to flow throughout. Alternating indoor and outdoor spaces attach to this stone spine beginning with a caretaker's apartment and terminating with a "glass box" living room hovering over the native landscape.

To relax the architectural rigor and to bring discoveries of nature into the complex, a wandering landscape path was configured to penetrate the stone spine and connect various outdoor spaces.

Angled window projections, raw steel columns, and connective detail are modernist contrasts to a stone wall.

Ryan Residence

SNOWMASS VILLAGE, COLORADO

This house celebrates the sights and sounds of water. A mountain stream flowing through the site becomes part of the home, beginning at the entry where it crosses under a bridge. The main living space, a glass-walled pavilion, engages the stream to the south and mountains to the north. Sunlight flashes off the water and fills the room with reflected light; terrace doors open to the sound of water tumbling over rocks.

The architecture explores a series of contrasts. Stone masses anchor a winged roof floating over the living room, emphasizing the light, airy qualities of the space. The exposed steel structure and zinc roof contrast with the textural qualities of the stone and wood siding. "Log chinking" recessed into wood siding gives visual strength to the walls and a somewhat tongue-in-cheek historic reference. The overall aesthetic is minimalist. In the clients' words: "we like a spare environment – it lets the people become important."

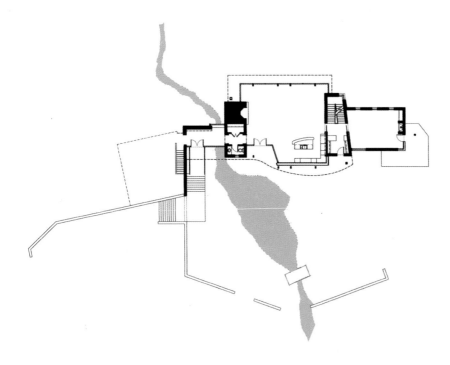

Coleman Ranch

RAVELLI COUNTY, MONTANA

Working closely with the owners' vision, the architects created a new form of Montana ranch emphasizing environmental stewardship.

Sited deep within a 1,200-acre parcel and situated on the edge of a commanding meadow, the ranch captures expansive mountain views as well as engaging the more intimate environment of river oxbow and riparian habitat. The compound is a carefully arranged ensemble of buildings comprising the main home, garage and guest wing, guest cabin, and "boy's club," a place for fly-tying, poker playing and tale-telling. Organized around an informal arrival courtyard, each building engages a different aspect of the site.

The home's contemporary ensemble of vernacular forms and textures blends seamlessly with the lowlands along the Bitterroot River. Drawing from images of western pole barns and rustic cabins, layers of local stone, log walls, timber and wood interact with large gestures of glass to engage the landscape. The interiors artfully blend western pieces with contemporary elements.

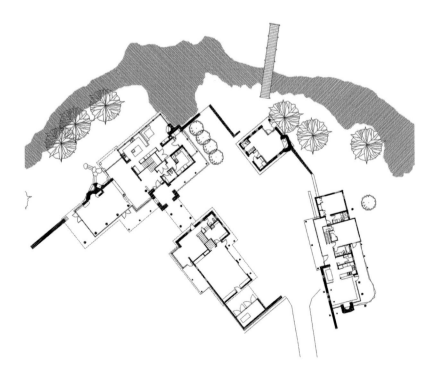

Vision Hill

TELLURIDE, COLORADO

This spectacular high country site looks at 360-degree panoramas of Telluride's vast mountainscape, yet it is completely treeless. To provide a sense of protection and intimacy, this house uses its own form to conceal, and then reveal, the expansive vistas. It claims small territories by enveloping outdoor spaces with distinct building masses.

The house is a series of "pods," choreographed to provide a sequence of experiences. Moving through the auto court and into the entry court, the forms of the house dominate and obscure most views. As one enters the house, two key vistas open up dramatically. Proceeding through the house, different scenes are revealed either as glimpses in transitional spaces or more fully in destination spaces.

The design avoids the overt western imagery often found in mountain homes. Instead, forms evolve organically from the landscape. Orientation to sun and topography helps ground the house, and the roof's deep eaves, sloping in response to angled walls, adds a complexity emphasizing the essence of "roof."

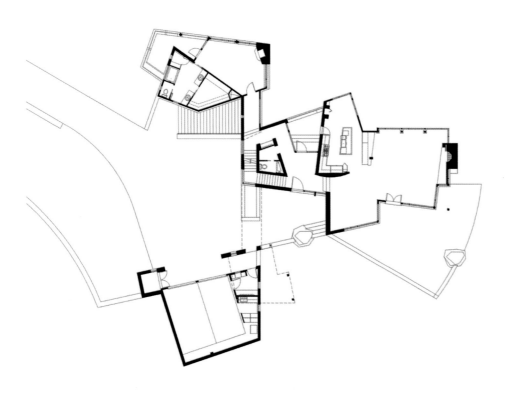

Warm natural materials – stone, wood, concrete and steel – and well-proportioned volumes provide a comfortable, elegant retreat.

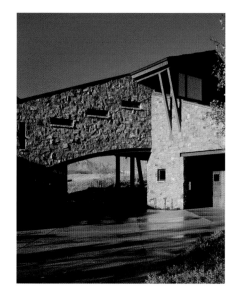

Architectural pods form distinct
spaces: the auto court leads under a
bridge into an entry court; a garden
court is adjacent to the living room.

80

Architects' Studio

BASALT, COLORADO

Three objectives guided the conception of the design studio: to physically manifest the firm culture of creativity and collaboration; to respond to its western small town neighborhood; and to be environmentally sensitive.

The unfussy "warehouse" interior works on many levels to satisfy the firm's core values. It allows for workspace flexibility when project teams change and it encourages the kind of casual encounters that foster collaboration. An outdoor deck and backyard patio offer additional gathering places and reflects the staff's passion for the outdoors. The unfinished interior also serves as a backdrop for the artifacts of creativity — drawings, models, material selections, and sketches — even art work from an extended family of friends and clients.

Contextually, the building expresses an energy sympathetic to its mainstreet neighbors. The studio components comply with town character: traditional western false front and simple materials, exhibited with a more modernist attitude.

Materials, such as stained concrete flooring, strawboard work stations, recycled carpet tiles, and native wood millwork minimize environmental impact. Off-the-shelf materials, like the production trusses in the main studio, contrast with one-of-a-kind pieces like the custom steel and stone reception desk, drawing attention to the inherent nature of each.

Decks, an outdoor conference room, and a backyard patio provide break-out space and reflect the firm's affinity for collaboration and nature.

Aspen Mountain Gondola

ASPEN, COLORADO

The gondola is the physical and symbolic link between the town of Aspen and Aspen Mountain. A community landmark in every sense, it is a draw for both visitors and locals alike. Located at the intersection of a central Aspen street and the gondola alignment up the mountain, the glass and steel box stands like a beacon, inviting passage to the top of Aspen Mountain's 11,212-foot summit.

Rendered in transparency, the building was envisioned as a display case, exposing skier activity and the complex machinery within. Its simplicity recalls the functional directness of Aspen's historic mining structures while its gable form echoes those of neighboring buildings.

The building sits on a two-tiered plaza, twenty-five paces from a lively après ski restaurant and bar, offering spectacular views and plenty of afternoon sun. The lower plaza, connected by a civic-scaled stair, opens to the street and accommodates skier arrival, skier services such as ticketing and ski school, and shopping. The diversity of amenities creates a hub of activity in all seasons.

Aspen Mountain's base development and gondola stand as enduring sources of civic pride. Conceived with broad community input, the process is lauded by local planning groups as an exemplary public-private partnership.

The Little Nell

ASPEN, COLORADO

The Little Nell provides a welcoming "front porch" for the community, linking the town center with the mountain base. Its completion redefined luxury lodging in mountain resorts.

Along with the Aspen Mountain Gondola, the hotel forms the heart of Aspen Mountain's base area redevelopment. The hotel's U-shaped mass forms a south-facing courtyard for hotel guests. Incorporating evergreen and aspen trees into the roof terraces, the courtyard provides privacy from nearby skier and pedestrian activity. On the outside of the "U," store fronts and pedestrian malls merge with the town fabric. The Little Nell is cited as a model of "sensitive large-scale development within a small-scale context."

The building reflects Aspen's heritage in both form and material. Red rose sandstone, used in historic civic buildings, is a primary material, rendered with rugged cleft faces or honed for emphasis. Most of the hotel's 92 rooms are one-of-a-kind. Roof spaces, typically unusable, become dormer rooms, guest favorites that are often booked months in advance.

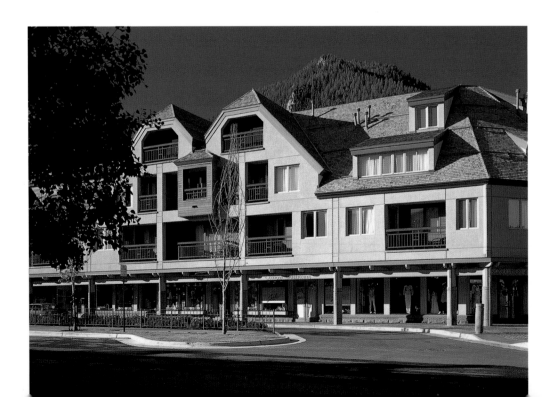

The landscaped courtyard is built over the parking garage and is the focus for public spaces.

Sundeck

ASPEN, COLORADO

Embodying ideas of sanctuary and refuge, this high-profile restaurant atop Aspen Mountain respectfully replaces an aging but historically important building.

The new building, which houses a full-service restaurant and bar, private club, ski school, and retail space needed to exemplify the Aspen Skiing Company's mission statement "to provide the opportunity for renewal of the human spirit" as well as its commitment to environmental stewardship. The Sundeck quickly met the challenge, becoming the place to meet, eat and celebrate on Aspen Mountain and passing the rigorous standards required by the U.S. Green Building Council for the Leadership in Energy and Environmental Design (LEED) certification — the only resort building to be recognized in 2000.

Set in an extreme alpine environment at 11,212-feet, the building's simple horizontal roofline gives it a quiet presence in contrast with the commanding geology of the mountain peaks around it. Its stone base grows out of the mountain bedrock foundation and the weathered-metal roof references the mountain's mining heritage.

A large stone hearth and copper clad fireplace, reminiscent of the original warming hut fireplace, is a physical gesture that honors the historic significance of Aspen's early years.

New Sheridan Restaurant

TELLURIDE, COLORADO

This lively bar and restaurant in the historic New Sheridan Hotel develops a dialogue between the character of the existing building and the more contemporary restaurant function. Material, color, and space planning generate a sequence of spaces with both modern and historical inflections.

Quiet curves and vigorous angles work together to contrast with the historic building's flat, rectilinear facade. The result is a dining atmosphere that acknowledges Telluride's past and future.

The architects selected all the interior finishes and furniture, enabling them to establish textural changes throughout the restaurant spaces. Materials provide warmth as well as historical nuance. Burnished galvanized zinc contrasts with patterned fabrics. The raw steel of the custom light fixtures hints at the local mining heritage while the cherry millwork is consistent with the hotel's interior vocabulary.

River Run Village at Keystone Resort

KEYSTONE, COLORADO

How can a "real place" be created in a resort setting when the marketplace endorses themed environments? River Run Village is the image center for a new resort community; the inaugural buildings embrace traditional associations of regional architecture while seeking to create new associations of western living.

Typical of the American West, the settlement history of Colorado includes simple ranch compounds, larger scaled American Rustic lodges, mining camps, and small, false-fronted towns. The village buildings liberally draw from these sources in a broad vernacular response with engaging historical associations. The straightforward, spare forms of early ranch settlements are interwoven with the exaggerated scale and craftsmanship characterizing the American Rustic tradition. An "exoskeleton" at the community icon recalls heavy boned mining structures.

Building shapes, materials and details are manipulated to form lively streets, gathering places, and residential units with great individuality. The architecture reflects the history of this valley and captures the energy of its future.

The buildings from a town square and main street; the tower is the village icon.

Residential decks and retail articulation engage the pedestrian streets, encouraging interaction and gathering.

The Aspen Club & Spa

ASPEN, COLORADO

The Aspen Club & Spa is designed as a prototype for a family of health retreats around the country reflecting the "Aspen Idea," an attitude promoting the revitalization of body, mind, and spirit first introduced by Walter Paepcke, a Chicago businessman and philanthropist who came to Aspen in 1949. This thinking expresses itself in the club in several ways.

The workout areas, with angled, muscular forms, strike a balance between energy and repose in the way boulders tumble in rock slides and come to rest with tension. The spa rooms exude calm and serenity through the careful use of color, light, materials, and sound. This dynamic interplay is accentuated in the palette of colors from Aspen's natural environment: sandstone reds, the yellows of fall aspens, and sunset oranges for the fitness rooms; and pale spruce greens in the spa. An interior waterfall visually connects to a natural stream framed through a window in a relaxation room, inviting the outdoors in.

Architectural details reinforce the integration of the natural world. A large skylight opens up to views of Aspen Mountain and creates a sense of place; handrails of pine saplings are reminiscent of tree branches; and naturally-toned woods echo the forested hillside.

Redstone Parkside

PARK CITY, UTAH

Redstone Parkside, a 750,000 sq. ft. mixed-use development near Park City, Utah, will create a new town center on the outskirts of an internationally acclaimed resort town. Surrounded by "rural sprawl," an outgrowth of Park City's popularity, Redstone Parkside seeks to unify and reinterpret the area's historical, cultural and social connections while creating an exciting environment for shopping, strolling, dining, outdoor activity, and living.

The community is anchored by the U.S. Ski and Snowboard Association's World Training Center and the Swaner Nature Preserve and Interpretive Center, and has expansive skyline views of three major ski resorts. Through the reinterpretation of vernacular architecture, the influence of the natural world in design and materials, and the introduction of a vibrant and diverse retail environment, the project will offer a compelling expression of modern mountain living.

The Inn at Semiahmoo

BLAINE, WASHINGTON

The commercial fishing heritage of the Northwest is well documented in legend and literature. The success of this 200-room resort hotel results from careful attention to site and heritage.

Formerly a salmon cannery, the site is now the heart of a resort retreat. It offers an 18-hole golf course, athletic facilities, entertainment and retail venues, a conference center, and marina with sea plane docking.

A vocabulary of forms and materials was inspired by the existing cannery buildings – industrial in use but with a direct, approachable, and comfortable architectural expression. The Inn encloses space within simple rhythmic volumes. Detailing is equally direct, with exposed chimney flues and welded wire handrails. Spareness carries through to the color scheme, a muted, monochromatic palette echoing the Northwest's weather.

Falling Leaf Lodge and the Chautauqua Center

MOUNTAIN AIR COUNTRY CLUB, BURNSVILLE, NORTH CAROLINA

Mountain Air Country Club is a golf community perched on a 4,700-ft peak in the Blue Ridge Mountains. The centerpieces for the community, Falling Leaf Lodge and the Chautauqua Center, also house everyday functions – post office, grocery store, children's and teen center, pro shop, and community living room.

The architecture reflects the cultural geography of Yancey County: living outdoors is delightful; nature has a strong presence; community gathering is important; arts and crafts are an integral part of history; and painted rural farmhouses and tobacco sheds are a striking built heritage.

These traits are embodied in three ways. The American Rustic tradition reflects the site's strong, natural character in an informal way, emphasizing natural materials, individuality and craftsmanship. The American Arts and Crafts Movement inspires a crafted functionalism where artistic interpretation and whimsy are embraced. And, indigenous vernacular is reinterpreted: painted clapboard and wooden "tobacco screens" are used where their strong color and dramatic detailing combine to create memorable spaces.

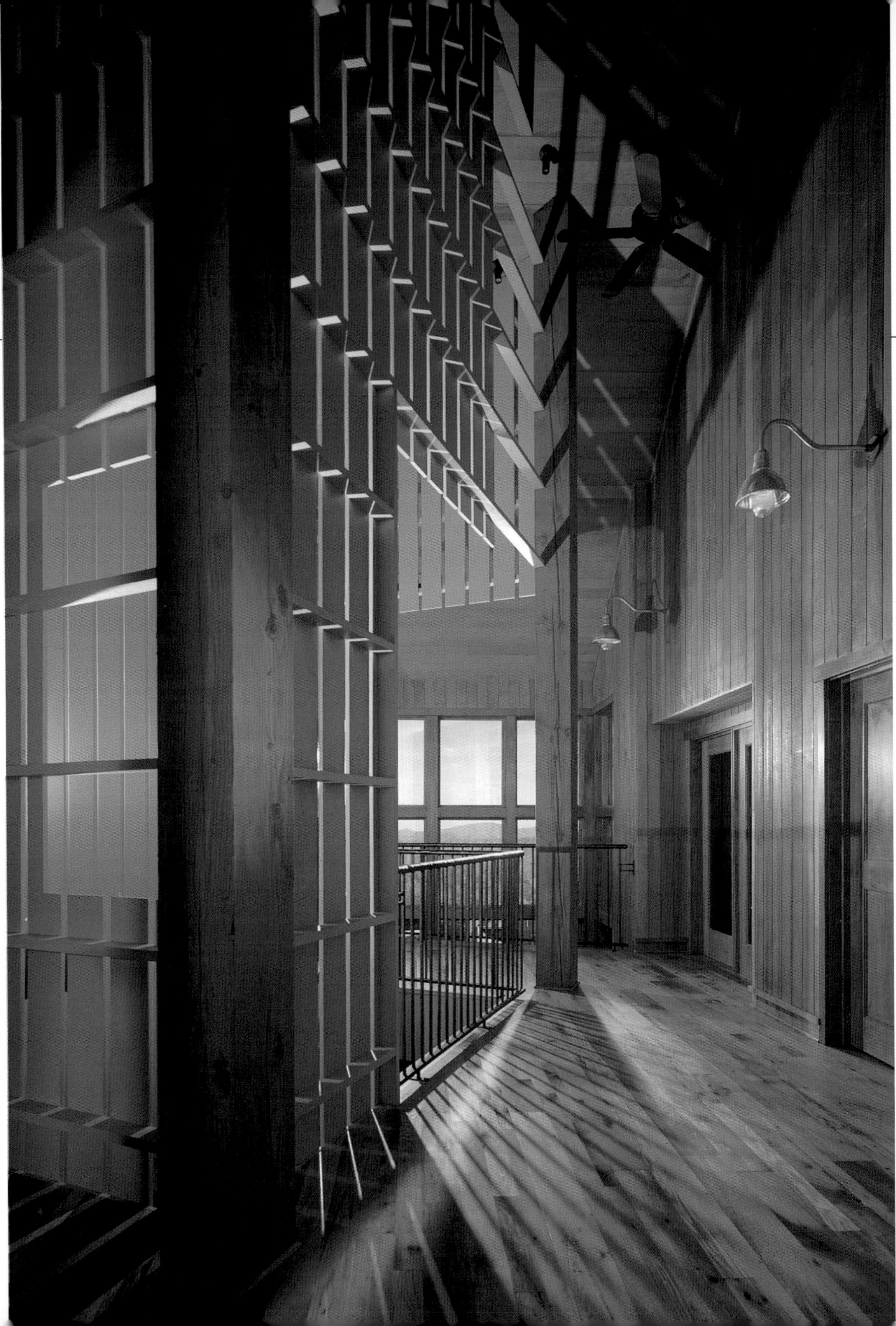

The architecture takes inspiration from North Carolina heritage, expressed in details such as painted clapboard and spaced wood siding.

121

Zephyr Mountain Lodge

WINTER PARK, COLORADO

The powerful myth of Winter Park's railroad heritage and the dominating presence of the surrounding mountains informed the vision for the Village at Winter Park as a civilized outpost on the edge of the Rocky Mountain wilderness. The village was conceived as a whole; individual buildings will be executed over time.

Perceived from a distance, the village appears to be cohesive – a closely knit cluster of buildings tucked into the mountain valley. At pedestrian level, the buildings create a series of carefully articulated vistas, streetscapes, and gathering spaces of great individuality.

Zephyr Mountain Lodge fronts a large plaza at the base of the mountain. Conceived as a "landmark in the landscape," its large size is given scale and texture with upper level "skyboxes" and anchoring elements on the lower floors. Street level building elements are the most highly detailed and expressive, creating a pedestrian experience with great vitality.

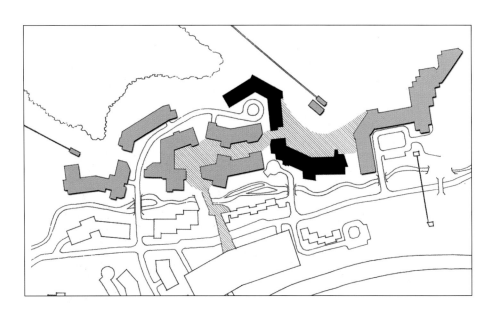

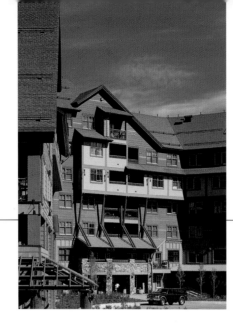

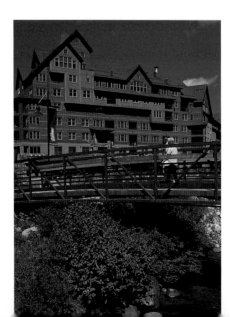

Firm History

126

Principals
John Cottle
Doug Graybeal
Larry Yaw
Richard Carr

Former Principals
Jim Copland
David Finholm
Tim Hagman
Mark Henthorn
Michael Thompson

Associates
Hans Berglund
Robert Schiller
Chris Touchette
Susan Touchette

Staff
Kenneth Bridges
Huey-Ru Chang
Ann Darby
Kim Doose
Andrew Evans
Cheryl Haynes
Mark Hardeman
Todd Kennedy
Jeffrey Klein
Alex Klumb
Matt Lee
Janet Leverson

Jeff McCollum
Scott McHale
Susan Nicholson
Jennifer Olson
Brian Paddack
Kyle Page
Karen Peterson
Duncan Porteous
Fiona Porteous
Michael Pritchard
Peter Sante
John Schenck
Steven Scollo
Chad Weltzin

Former Staff
Eric Aanonsen
Susan Abel
Malinda Allison
Ben Anderson
Erik Anderson
Colleen Avery
John Backman
Robert Bauman
Philip Beck
James Benjamin
Tracey Black
Madelyn Blumenthal
Sue Bonet
Colin Brice
Barbara Britz

Brandon Burns
Michael Carpenter
Jennifer Carr
Cowan Chang
Scott Christensen
Monique Coe
Barbara Courtney
Jessica Coyle
Lorie D'Alessio
Renee Dake
David Damon
Michael Doyle
Shannon Doyle
Laura Dwyer
Rose Eberli
Nicki Finholm
Laura Grafel
Stephanie Grandjacques
Bruce Gray
Gretchen Greenwood
Mike Hamberg
Nils Hammerbeck
Jim Hardy
Lynn Hardy
Kellie Hassinger
Debbie Hembel
Kristine Hengy
Jerry Hobgood
Heidi Hoffman
Mary Holley
Dale Hoover

John Houldin
Keith Howie
Christopher Jahn
Oli Johansson
Dylan Johns
Karen Johnson
Tim Keiffer
Beth Knudson
Kip Kummer
Brian Kwekel
Lisa LaGuardia
Emily Lawson
Erik Lind
Jerry Logan
Debra Lujan
Carrie McIntyre
Eileen McIntyre
Cat McMenimen
Holly MacDonald
William Maron
Martin Mata
Caleb Mulvena
Jordan Neal
Bjorn Nelson
Joe Neys
Jaime Olson
Melinda Pearson
Deborah Pease
Charles Pederson
Michelle Petruno
Dave Polich

Michael Pukas
Graham Reed
Chris Ridings
Dave Ritchie
Charles Rosenberg
Les Rosenstein
Jerry Ross
Mark Rudolf
Will Saltonstall
Laura Schappert
Chrystl Schuster
Charles Schwab
Robert Sharp
B.J. Smith
Theresa Snyder
Jill Spaeh
Wayne Stryker
Reggie Stump
Pamela Sudmeier
Thamronkeat Supawit
George Switzer
Peter Szczelina
Lisa Teal
Karrie Tenley
Andrew Thompson
Michael Thompson
Anna Timroth
Matthew Tracy
Robert Trimble
Doug Unfug
Do-Yong Um

Jason Upper
Sheri Vail
Jake Vickery
Anne Wachsler
Ken Wells
John Wheeler
Brian Wilson
Steve Wilson
Julie Woodruff
Troy Worgull
Jodie Wright
Ron Yaw

Acknowledgements

SOPRIS MOUNTAIN RANCH Emma, Colorado
Client: Private
Contractor: Wood Construction, Inc.
Awards:
Colorado West Chapter AIA Honor Award 1991
AIA Western Mountain Region Honor Award 1992

MINTZ RESIDENCE Vail, Colorado
Client: Alan and Ann Mintz
Contractor: Beck and Associates
Photographer: Pat Sudmeier
Awards:
Colorado West Chapter AIA Merit Award 2001

PRIVATE RESIDENCE Aspen, Colorado
Client: Private
Contractor: Todd Habermann Construction
Interior Designer: Constance Noah
Landscape Architect: Design Workshop, Inc.
Photographer: David O. Marlow
Awards:
Colorado West Chapter AIA Honor Award 1996
The Chicago Athenaeum: Museum of Architecture and
Design, American Architecture Awards 1998
Steve Dach Architectural Excellence, Grand Award 2000

PRIVATE RESIDENCE Telluride, Colorado
Client: Private
Contractor: Dennis Overly
Photographer: David O. Marlow

CASTLE CREEK RESIDENCE Aspen, Colorado
Client: Private
Contractor: Todd Habermann Construction
Photographer: David O. Marlow
Awards:
Colorado Society of Architects Design Award 1980
NIKKEI Architecture Design Award 1980

RAMO RESIDENCE Eagle County, Colorado
Client: John and Jolie Ramo
Contractor: Graber Construction
Photographer: Douglas Kahn
Awards:
Colorado West Chapter AIA Honor Award 1998

PINON MESA HOMESTEAD Southern Colorado
Client: Private
Photographer: Pat Sudmeier

HOUSE AT WILDCAT RIDGE
Snowmass Village, Colorado
Client: Private
Contractor: Todd Habermann Construction
Interior Designer: Associates III
Photographer: J. Curtis

PRIVATE RESIDENCE Boulder, Colorado
Client: Private
Contractor: Rob Luckett Construction Company
Interior Designer: Associates III
Photographer: David O. Marlow

POWELL RESIDENCE Telluride, Colorado
Client: Ned and Diane Powell
Contractor: Wodehouse Builders
Photographer: Jim Christy/Larry Yaw
Awards:
AIA Colorado Honor Award 1998
AIA Colorado Architects Choice Award 1998

WRIGHT RESIDENCE Snowmass Village, Colorado
Client: Robert and Susanne Wright
Contractor: Norris and Associates
Interior Designer: Suzy Knezevich
Photographer: J Curtis/John Cottle

PRIVATE RESIDENCE Eagle County, Colorado
Client: Private
Contractor: George Schaeffer Construction Company
Interior Designer: Design Coalition
Landscape Architect: Land Designs by Ellison

SCHELL RESIDENCE Telluride, Colorado
Client: Rick and Barbara Schell
Contractor: Overly Construction
Photographer: Douglas Kahn

SOPRIS DRIVE RESIDENCE Basalt, Colorado
Client: Private
Contractor: Courtney Construction
Photographer: Pat Sudmeier

SMITHBURG RESIDENCE Aspen, Colorado
Client: Bill and Maria Smithburg
Contractor: Todd Habermann Construction
Interior Designer: R. Pearlman Designs
Landscape Architect: Maria Smithburg
Photographer: Larry Yaw

RYAN RESIDENCE Snowmass Village, Colorado
Client: Jim and Colleen Ryan
Contractor: Todd Habermann Construction
Landscape Architect: Mt. Daly Enterprises

COLEMAN RESIDENCE Ravelli County, Montana
Client: Lew & Suzie Coleman
Contractor: Hammer Power Corporation
Interior Designer: Luis Ortega Design Studio
Landscape Architect: Todd R. Cole Landscape
Architecture
Photographer: David O. Marlow

VISION HILL Telluride, Colorado
Client: Private
Contractor: James Hughes Construction
Landscape Architect: Kristin Surette
Interior Designer: Studio Frank
Photographer: David O. Marlow

ARCHITECTS' STUDIO Basalt, Colorado
Client: Toree Associates, LLC
Contractor: B&H General Contractors
Landscape Architect: Mt. Daly Enterprises
Photographer: Pat Sudmeier
Awards:
Colorado West Chapter AIA Citation Award 2000
Gold Nugget Grand Award 2000
ASID Colorado, Green Design Award 2001
AIA Colorado Citation Award 2001

ASPEN MOUNTAIN GONDOLA Aspen, Colorado
Client: Aspen Skiing Company
Contractor: Shaw Construction
Planning/Landscape Architect: Design Workshop, Inc.
Photographer: J Curtis
Awards:
Colorado West Chapter AIA Honor Award 1987
Colorado West Chapter AIA Honor Award 1987
Urban Land Institute Award of Excellence 1995

THE LITTLE NELL Aspen, Colorado
Client: Aspen Skiing Company
Contractor: Shaw Construction
Planning/Landscape Architect: Design Workshop, Inc.
Photographer: David O. Marlow
Awards:
ULI Award for Excellence Mixed-Use Facilities 1990
National Ski Area Award Best Lodge 1990
Best Inn, Snow Country Design Awards 1991

SUNDECK Aspen, Colorado
Client: Aspen Skiing Company
Contractor: Shaw Construction
Landscape Architect: Design Workshop, Inc.
Photographer: Pat Sudmeier
Awards:
U.S. Green Building Council Leadership in Energy and
Environmental Design (LEED) Certification 2000

NEW SHERIDAN RESTAURANT Telluride, Colorado
Client: Leucadia Financial Corporation
Contractor: Shaw Construction
Photographers: Chris Morona/Chris Travis

RIVER RUN VILLAGE AT KEYSTONE RESORT
Keystone, Colorado
Client: Keystone Real Estate Development, LLC
Contractor: Weitz-Cohen Construction Company

Planning/Landscape Architect: Eldon Beck & Associates
Photographers: Douglas Kahn/ J. Curtis
Awards:
Gold Nugget Merit Award,
Best Community Site Plan 1997

Black Bear Lodge:
Steve Dach Architectural Excellence Merit Award 1996
Gold Nugget Merit Award,
Best Mixed-Use Project 1997

Jackpine Lodge:
AIA Colorado Merit Award 1997

Silver Mill:
AIA Colorado Honor Award 1998
Colorado West Chapter AIA Honor Award 1998
Gold Nugget Merit Award,
Best Mixed-Use Project 1998

ASPEN CLUB Aspen, Colorado
Client: The Fox Companies
Contractor: Rudd Construction
Landscape Architect: Design Workshop, Inc.
Photographers: David O. Marlow/Pat Sudmeier

REDSTONE PARKSIDE Park City, Utah
Client: MJM Neighborhood Builders
Planning: Design Workshop, Inc.

INN AT SEMIAHMOO Blaine, Washington
Client: The Semiahmoo Company
Contractor: Koll International
Design Architect/Architect of Record:
Callison Architecture, Inc.
Photographer: Larry Yaw
Awards:
Colorado West Chapter AIA Honor Award 1987
AIA Colorado Honor Award 1987

FALLING LEAF LODGE and the CHAUTAUQUA
CENTER
Mountain Air Country Club, Burnsville, North Carolina
Client: Randy and Jeannie Banks
Contractor: Miller Building Corporation
Interior Designer: The Ranch House
Landscape Architect: Scott Melrose & Associates, PA
Photographer: Robert Thien

ZEPHYR MOUNTAIN LODGE Winter Park, Colorado
Client: Hines Interests Limited Partnership
Contractor: Mortensen
Interior Designer: J. Kattman Associates
Planning/Landscape Architect: Design Workshop, Inc.
Photographers: Douglas Kahn/Michael Shopenn